W9-CTI-054

COMMUNITY HELPERS

Construction Workers

by Chris Bowman

BELLWETHER MEDIA • MINNEAPOLIS, MN

Note to Librarians, Teachers, and Parents:

Blastoff! Readers are carefully developed by literacy experts and combine standards-based content with developmentally appropriate text.

Level 1 provides the most support through repetition of high-frequency words, light text, predictable sentence patterns, and strong visual support.

Level 2 offers early readers a bit more challenge through varied simple sentences, increased text load, and less repetition of high-frequency words.

Level 3 advances early-fluent readers toward fluency through increased text and concept load, less reliance on visuals, longer sentences, and more literary language.

Level 4 builds reading stamina by providing more text per page, increased use of punctuation, greater variation in sentence patterns, and increasingly challenging vocabulary.

Level 5 encourages children to move from "learning to read" to "reading to learn" by providing even more text, varied writing styles, and less familiar topics.

Whichever book is right for your reader, Blastoff! Readers are the perfect books to build confidence and encourage a love of reading that will last a lifetime!

This edition first published in 2018 by Bellwether Media, Inc.

No part of this publication may be reproduced in whole or in part without written permission of the publisher. For information regarding permission, write to Bellwether Media, Inc., Attention: Permissions Department, 5357 Penn Avenue South, Minneapolis, MN 55419.

Library of Congress Cataloging-in-Publication Data

Names: Bowman, Chris, 1990- author.
Title: Construction Workers / by Chris Bowman.
Description: Minneapolis, MN : Bellwether Media, Inc., 2018. | Series: Blastoff! Readers: Community Helpers | Includes bibliographical references and index. | Audience: Ages 5-8. | Audience: K to Grades 3.
Identifiers: LCCN 2017035844 (print) | LCCN 2017037626 (ebook) | ISBN 9781626177437 (hardcover : alk. paper) | ISBN 9781681034980 (ebook)
Subjects: LCSH: Building–Juvenile literature. | Construction workers–Juvenile literature.
Classification: LCC TH149 (ebook) | LCC TH149 .B69 2018 (print) | DDC 690–dc23
LC record available at https://lccn.loc.gov/2017035844

Text copyright © 2018 by Bellwether Media, Inc. BLASTOFF! READERS and associated logos are trademarks and/or registered trademarks of Bellwether Media, Inc. SCHOLASTIC, CHILDREN'S PRESS, and associated logos are trademarks and/or registered trademarks of Scholastic Inc., 557 Broadway, New York, NY 10012.

Editor: Nathan Sommer   Designer: Brittany McIntosh

Printed in the United States of America, North Mankato, MN.

Table of Contents

Robert is building a new house. He carries wood to his work area.

Robert builds
a wall with his
hammer and nails.
The house will be
ready soon!

What Are Construction Workers?

Construction workers build roads and bridges. They also make buildings.

They work at **construction sites**. Sites are found in both big cities and small towns.

construction site

What Do Construction Workers Do?

Construction workers first **prepare** their site. They make sure everything is safe.

They clean the area. Then, they move **materials** for the **project**.

Construction workers have a lot of gear. Small tools and big machines help them build.

Construction Worker Gear

hard hat

safety glasses

tool belt

hammer

17

What Makes a Good Construction Worker?

Construction workers are strong. These workers lift heavy objects often.

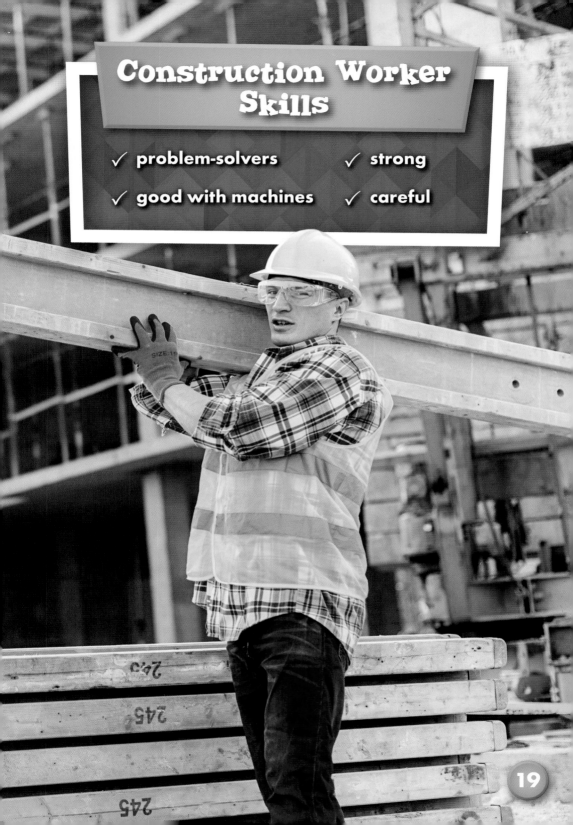

Construction Worker Skills

✓ problem-solvers ✓ strong

✓ good with machines ✓ careful

19

They are also careful.
Construction workers
build our world!

Glossary

construction sites

places where construction workers build projects

prepare

to get ready

materials

things that are used to help make something else

project

a building, road, or bridge that construction workers build

To Learn More

AT THE LIBRARY

Less, Emma. *Construction Workers*. Mankato, Minn.: Amicus Ink, 2018.

Meister, Cari. *Construction Workers*. Minneapolis, Minn.: Bullfrog Books, 2015.

Waldendorf, Kurt. *Hooray for Construction Workers!* Minneapolis, Minn.: Lerner Publications, 2017.

ON THE WEB

Learning more about construction workers is as easy as 1, 2, 3.

1. Go to www.factsurfer.com.

2. Enter "construction workers" into the search box.

3. Click the "Surf" button and you will see a list of related web sites.

With factsurfer.com, finding more information is just a click away.

Index

The images in this book are reproduced through the courtesy of: Dmitry Kalinovsky, front cover, pp. 16-17; Jozef Sowa, pp. 2-3; sirtravelalot, pp. 4-5, 6-7; Chris Sattlberger/ Alamy, pp. 8-9; Hung Chung Chih, pp. 10-11; sturti/ Getty Images, pp. 12-13; Aisyaqilumaranas, pp. 14-15, 22 (bottom left); tankist276, p. 17 (safety glasses); ifong, p. 17 (tool belt); Stockforlife, p. 17 (hard hat); Paket, p. 17 (hammer); Drazen Lovric, pp. 18-19; humphery, pp. 20-21; Perfect Gui, p. 22 (top left); Monkey Business Images, p. 22 (top right); mdgn, p. 22 (bottom right).